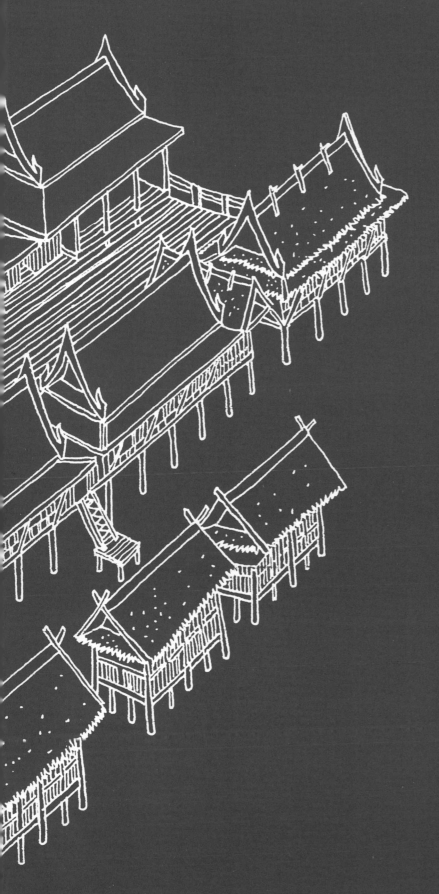

Old Homes of Bangkok

Fragile Link

Old Homes of Bangkok

Fragile Link

Text and Photographs by
Barry Michael Broman
With a foreward by
M.R. Kukrit Pramoj

DD Books
Bangkok

The Siam Society
Bangkok

Published by:
The Siam Society
Under Royal Patronage
131 Soi Asoke
Bangkok 10110, Thailand.
DD Books
32/9-10 Soi Asoke
Bangkok 10110, Thailand
First published in 1984
Printed at Aksorn Samphan Press, Thailand.

Broman, Barry Michael
Old Homes of Bangkok, Fragile Link
ISBN 974-8614-60-3

for B.J.

Maps of Bangkok 1897

Acknowledgements

I must first thank all the owners or tenants of the houses pictured in this book for their cooperation and hospitality in letting me into their homes. I am especially grateful to Her Majesty Queen Rambhai Barni for permitting me to photograph her home, Sukhothai Palace.

Persons who have helped and encouraged me on this venture are too numerous to mention individually. Some who have provided special and much appreciated assistance include: Miss Pranalee Singara na Ayudhya, M.C. Subhatradis Disakul, Wing Commander Sudhi Lekhananda, Miss Victoria Butler, and my colleagues Mr. Timothy Michael Carney and Mr. David Spillane.

A word of great appreciation must be expressed to Mrs. Jacqueline Page Sutliffe and Mr. Nit Ratanasanya for their many hours of work in the layout and design of this work and to Dr. Sumet Jumsai na Ayudhya for his help in the design.

My thanks go to M.R. Kukrit Pramoj for contributing the forward of this book.

Finally, I pay homage to the memory of two long-time residents of Siam, Rudolf Hampe and Theo Meier, both artists, whose appreciation and application of the fine art of living in the traditional Thai manner first caused me to become interested in this subject.

Foreword

To write a foreword to a book is, I suppose, to agree with and approve of the book. As a resident of Bangkok and a descendant of many long-dead masterminds who built the city, this book has certainly increased both my already overflowing pride and embarassment.

The original builders of Bangkok certainly had the old capital, Ayudhya, in mind when they first laid down the plans. However, they had confidence in themselves and felt sure that they could prevent it from sharing the same fate as the old capital. They also laid down strategic plans to defend the city from afar so that no enemy could ever come within sight of the city walls. If they had not done this they would not have built the Golden Mount, which could very well serve as a base for enemy artillery, so near the city wall as to overlook it.

The builders of Bangkok, having such confidence in themselves, also had great ambitions. They were determined to build a Greater Ayudhya, as the term Mahindra-yudhaya in Bangkok's official title implies.

This brings us to another point of fact about Bangkok. It is the only city in the world that has been ennobled and given a long title. It was born with the name of Bangkok, of course, but since it became the Royal City, it was ennobled and given, like any Thai who has been in royal service, the title of Krung Sri Ratanakosindra - The Royal City of the Green Jewel, linking it with the Emerald Buddha, with many other honorifics to follow.

Defensive strategy seemed to be, as well, behind the development of Bangkok in the reigns of King Mongkut and King Chulalongkorn. Western colonialism was then rampant in this part of the world. Western imperialists often declared that their reason for colonizing a country was to give it western civilization, which was at that period accepted as the only civilization in the world and could be used as an excuse for all kinds of atrocities.

King Mongkut and King Chulalongkorn preempted western colonization by, as it were, colonizing Siam themselves. That is to say they began to build in the country, especially in Bangkok, a western architectural façade, behind which the old and original Siam hid itself. Western fashion in hairstyle and dress was adopted; mandarins were moved from their homes to work in western-looking ministries with real desks and chairs; instead of crouching on the floor in the presence of royalty they were forced, on pain of dire punishment, to stand upright; polygamy disguised as ladies-in-waiting or maids of honour to the chief wife, who was the only one to be introduced to western visitors. Thus a completely already-colonized western atmosphere was established.

It was a lovely chimera but it did not matter, because it was convincing and Siam remains uncolonized down to this day.

This book is a testimony to the brave efforts of our remarkable and colourful Thai V.I.P.s of the past, who succeeded in keeping this country afloat and independent.

We, of the present generation, have certainly made a mess of their chief handiwork, Bangkok. But again it does not matter or mai pen rai, since we are still thankful to them for having preserved for us the independence to make a mess of things.

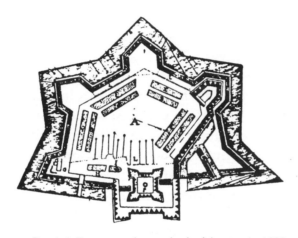

Bangkok Fortress on the east bank of the river in 1688.

Fragile Link: Old Homes of Bangkok

It would be difficult to imagine a worse site for a national capital of six million people than that selected by the founding fathers of Bangkok. However there were compelling reasons for choosing this small village on the Chao Phraya River whose name translates as "the village of the wild plum". A former capital at Ayudhya, just sixty kilometers to the north, was sacked and burned by the Burmese in 1767. The capital was then shifted to Thonburi located on the west bank of the Chao Phraya River opposite Bangkok which was at the time a small fishing village and the home of some Chinese merchants. In 1782, shortly after General Chakri assumed power by concensus and founded his new ruling dynasty (of which the present king, His Majesty King Bhumibol Adulyadej, is the ninth regnant), he moved the capital from Thonburi to Bangkok. The new site had marshy terrain to the east and the river to the west for better protection against possible Burmese attacks. Here Rama I (Chakri kings are considered the incarnations of Vishnu and therefore are known as Rama) commenced building his new capital in the image of the destroyed Ayudhya. The Grand Palace was begun the following year and the new city was christened "Ratanakosindr"--Jewel Abode of the God Indra. Rama I's military intuition proved correct; the Burmese invaded four times during his reign.

The Chakri kings flourished in Bangkok building many fine palaces, homes, and temples with zeal, skill, and devotion. Eventually western technicians, including architects, were introduced to assist in the design and construction of many of the new works. At the same time promising Siamese (the Kingdom was not known as Thailand until 1939) were sent abroad for education. Others studied Western ideas and designs in Bangkok, especially during the reigns of Rama IV (known in the West as Mongkut) and Rama V (Chulalongkorn), the great innovators of the dynasty. The result was a blend of European and Siamese architecture, often executed in a delightfully eclectic fashion. The Chakri Throne Hall inside the Grand Palace is a good example, designed originally in the nineteenth century by the Italian Rigotti. Conservative

advisors to King Chulalongkorn wanted the building to have some aspects of Siamese design. Thus three ornate pagoda-like spires were grafted to the otherwise Western - styled building. The result was charming, stately, and "modern" as the times demanded, but also distinctively Siamese. Today the Chakri Throne Hall is used by His Majesty for state ceremonies and dinners.

Western ideas and technology began to enter the Kingdom in earnest in the mid-nineteenth century and set the course towards modernization which Thailand follows to this day. The style of living in those times was reflected in the popularity of Victorian architecture among the gentry. Some modifications were necessary to accommodate the architecture of Europe to pre-airconditioned Siam. Happily the changes were usually successful, albeit sometimes strange, in the characteristic Siamese pattern of selecting the best of alien cultures and adapting them to local tastes and needs.

This is not to suggest that Bangkok was festooned with semi-European style buildings at the turn of the century. Far from it. The city was predominately Asian in appearance, style, and temperament and retained this charm until after the Second World War when it began the rapid expansion which has made it - - for better or worse - - the metropolis of today.

Most of the houses of Bangkok were simple wooden structures with sharply angled roofs. They were built off the ground on sturdy piles and were located most of the time near the ubiquitous klongs (canals) which served as the city's primary thorofares. The many klongs of the city caused Bangkok to be dubbed by generations of travel writers the "Venice of the East" with gradually diminishing truth. Lush tropical trees and vegetation abounded, and Bangkok gardens were wild, aromatic scenes of color and shade. In 1864 New Road, the city's first road, was completed near the river; formerly it had been an elephant track. Other streets followed capped by Rajadamnoen Avenue, planned by King Chulalongkorn as Siam's answer to the Champs Elysées

Floating houses along the river at Bangkok.
From "Siam, das Reich des weissen Elephanten"
Ernst von Hesse Wartegg, Leipzig 1899

and Pall Mall. His Majesty laid out roads and decreed that trees should line them. "My people shall walk in the shade", he said. As roads came klongs went. Few survive to-day and most of those that remain are dangerously (and odoriferously) polluted. There are, however, some charming small klongs on the outskirts of the city which serve as a reminder of what the city must once have been like.

Probably the best known "house on a klong" in Bangkok is that of the late American silk manufacturer James Thompson, who mysteriously disappeared in 1966 while vacationing in Malaysia. A resident of Siam since the end of the Second World War, Thompson resurrected the Thai silk industry and assembled a renowned Asian art collection. Some say his finest deed, however, was to construct his Thai-style house composed of parts of several old houses from Bangkok and the provinces which were dismantled and re-assembled in the Thompson compound on the banks of Klong Maha Nag. Today the house is open to the public and is administered by the James Thompson Foundation which preserves the house and its celebrated art collection.

Many of the fine Thai style houses in Bangkok were not originally constructed in the city, but were brought from "up country" and reconstructed on their present sites. A good example is Suan Pakkad Palace where resides Princess Chumbhot of Nagara Svarga, surrounded by several beautiful old buildings including the famed "lacquer pavilion". Tula Bunnag has reasssembled four old houses from Ayudhya province forming them in the shape of a quadrangle with an elevated deck connecting them. Situated on a klong on the outskirts of Bangkok, the house sits in stark contrast to the concrete and glass residences of the suburbs. Former prime minister M.R. Kukrit Pramoj has made his home in a grouping of old houses reconstructed on his spacious grounds at Suan Phlu. The highlight of this ensemble is a 170-year old sala (reception hall or room) which M.R. Kukrit uses to receive guests whom he considers worthy of the treat. A classic example of northern Thai architecture is the Kamthieng House, located on the grounds of the Siam Society on Soi Asoke. At one time the residence of members of

A floating house in Bangkok.
From : "Siam, das Reich....."

the Nimmanheminda family of Chiang Mai, in the middle of the nineteenth century,
the house actually a series of small buildings came to Bangkok through the generosity
of the family and a series of grants.

Unlike the west where dismantling a house is a difficulty, often impossible task,
traditional Thai houses are built to be taken down and moved. The houses are often
built in standard sizes so that parts of one can be fitted to another. The ease of dismantling is facilitated by the minimal use of nails; fine joining and the use of wooden
pegs in construction not only make the houses more aesthetically appealing but also
easier and cheaper to move. The use of teakwood as a construction material explains
why many of the remaining houses in the city have survived the rigors of tropical heat,
monsoon rains, and hungry insects. Teak can last for centuries if properly cared for.

The sad fact is that Bangkok has few old Thai style houses remaining. The enormous
change that the city has seen in recent decades does not fully explain this phenomonon.
Bangkok's relative youth as a major city, and the strong European architectural influences
on the city beginning a century ago prevented many traditional type homes from even
being built, especially by the well-to-do families. Only in recent years has there been
a renaissance among Bangkokians to construct Thai style residences in the city.

Most of the stately homes of the city are built in a colonial style which was
popular throughout most of Southeast Asia around the turn of the century. At that time
Bangkok had about 350,000 people and the small European community was largely
centered along the river or on Sathorn Road. Silom Road (Windmill Road) had klongs
on both sides when elephants and carriages began to give way to motor cars. King
Chulalongkorn used to drive down Rajadamnoen Avenue (The Royal Way) in his yellow
electric auto. One of Bangkok's doyenne Europeans, Irmgaard Eisenhofer, recalls the
rickshaw boys at the Oriental Hotel knowing the homes of all the European residents
of Bangkok; ceiling punkahs pulled by small boys and hidden out of sight, and dinner
parties where women were given pillow cases to guard their feet against mosquitoes.

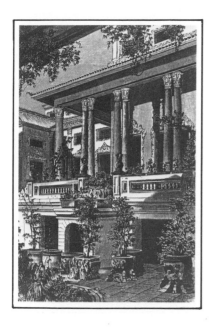

The Palace of the King of Siam, Bangkok.
From "Sia , the Land
of the hite Elephant…"

Perhaps the best colonial architecture in Siam (which was never colonized) is reflected in several of the older embassy residences in Bangkok. In consideration for assistance during wars with the Burmese, the Portuguese were given a choice parcel of land on the east bank of the river in 1786, four years after the founding of the city as the capital. The present Portuguese Embassy is located on a piece of land given to Portugal in 1820. It is the oldest and arguably the finest embassy residence in the city. Further down the river sits the French Embassy, another reminder of how pleasant life along the river must have been a century ago. The British forsook the river in the early 1920's when they shifted their embassy to the wilds and wide open spaces of Ploenchit Road. Today Queen Victoria's statue looks out upon an endless stream of vehicles which creep past the Embassy at one of Bangkok's prime traffic bottle-necks.

Considering their numbers and influence in Siam the Chinese are under-represented in terms of architecture. Many Chinese temples can be found in Bangkok, especially in the predominately Chinese section of town called Yaowarat, but there are few old residences in the Chinese style. Among the finest of these is the house built about 1882 for Phraya Phisol Sombat Boribul. Ironically it was designed by a European who somewhat blended Chinese with Western architectural styles. Another fine Chinese house, located on Sathorn Road, is the Hok Lok Siaw House of Lalong Bunnag. Built around 1813, the house was first located near the river. It was moved to its present site late in the nineteenth century and was modified by a French engineer in 1892.

A residence which might be more at home in Milan of Florence is Ban Tom Sin, or as it is more commonly known, Ban Phitsanuloke, on Phitsanuloke Road. This Italian-style mansion was a gift of Rama VI to Phraya Anirut Deva, one of his favorites at court. Looking like a richly ornate cake and set in a parklike compound replete with classic renaissance statuary, Ban Tom Sin now belongs to the government and is now the Prime Minister's official residence.

The old houses of Bangkok demand attention not merely because of the age

View of Bangkok in the 19th century.
From "Siam, das Reich......"

and beauty or because of the danger of their disappearance (although these are both valid reasons), but primarily they constitute a legacy and reflection of the countervailing historical and cultural influences that have shaped Bangkok. They chronicle the growth of the city as Siam became Thailand and as a feudal society was transformed to a constitutional monarchy.

The pressure of population, which has changed Bangkok from an undistinguished, bucolic Asian backwater town of a hundred years ago to a sprawling modern city of six million inhabitants today has been disastrous for the old homes. Many have been destroyed, sacrificed to the maw of modernity. Others survive in cramped compounds where once spacious gardens have been filled with smaller houses for younger generations. High rise apartments grow up, commercial centers appear, townhouses come into vogue. In every case old houses are torn down to make way for "progress". Perhaps this is as it should be. For a city to live it must grow and build and Bangkok is growing faster than most. But city planners have seen the negative effects of rapid urban growth and the results are not good. Bangkokians are looking more carefully at the value of rapid growth and change. Old values are remembered and resurrected. All to the good. If Bangkok is to retain any of its once famed charm and appeal, it will be necessary to preserve some of the elements which gave rise to the appeal. Preservation has begun, thanks in part to good works of the Association of Siamese Architects and partly to the efforts of men like Rolf von Büeren who have re-created traditional yet functional home in the center of a rapidly changing city.

This book seeks not to see Bangkok as it is but rather as it was. It pays tribute to the builders who gave Bangkok such a wealth of architectural innovation. And it celebrates those in Bangkok who appreciate the worth of these houses and seek their preservation.

16

Spirit house

River scene

House in China Town

Baskets on a woven tray

Window detail

19

Lekhyananda family at Petchaburi road

Klong jars.

Kamthieng House at Siam Society.

Jim Thompson House

Butterfly

Kamthieng House

Wooden wall detail

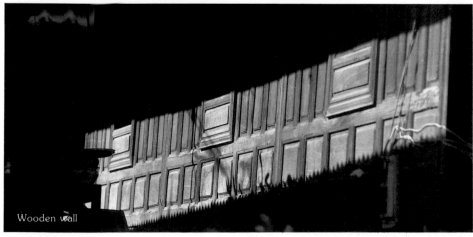

Wooden wall

23

Lacquer Pavilion at Suan Pakkad Palace

Klongs

The klong behind Jim Thompson House

Bangkok is built on marshes and transportation in the city has traditionally been water-borne. Today many of the ubiquitous canals, or klongs, have been filled in to provide space for roads but many klongs continue to serve around the city and especially in Bangkok's twin city Thonburi on the west bank of the Chao Phraya River. Here life is little changed from the days when Bangkok was dependent on her waterways.

Bath time

Paddling down the klong

Quiet klong

Longtail boat

Klong dweller

Family event

30

Rinse

Commerce on the klong

Old house in Thonburi

Play time   Cleaning up

House boat in the city at the turn of the century
(With kind permission of the National Library, Bangkok)

Pavilion on the klong

Suan Pakkad Palace

Several of the finest reconstructed Thai-style buildings in the city can be found at Suan Pakkad Palace, the home of Princess Chumbhot. This collection of meticulously restored building features the sublime Lacquer Pavilion and serves as home to an important art collection which is open to the public.

The Lacquer Pavilion

Resident pelican

The main house from the Lacquer Pavilion

The main house

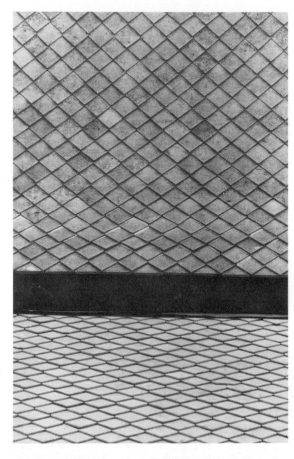

Roof detail

The Lacquer Pavilion
from the main house

Watch geese

Old Homes on Rajdamri Road

Several fine old homes survive on Rajdamri Road opposite the Royal Bangkok Sports Club. These houses were designed by Phraya Burutraj Rajavallop, the Chamberlain of Rama V (r. 1873-1910 AD), at the command of Rama VI (r. 1910-1925 AD) who had the houses constructed for rental to foreigners. The proceeds from these houses was a gift to the Royal Pages School which later became Vachiravut College, named for its royal benefactor.

Following the Second World War the United States Embassy obtained three of these houses, including the one pictured, to serve as residences for senior American diplomats assigned in Bangkok.

Close-up of the tower

From the driveway   Side view

Detail above entrance
of Bang Khun Prom Palace.

Bang Khun Prom Palace

The German architect Karl Döring designed this baroque style residence on the banks of the Chao Phraya River for Prince Paribatra of Nagara Svarga, a son of King Rama V. Following the 1932 coup which ended the absolute monarchy in Siam, Prince Paribatra was exiled and spent the rest of his life abroad. His residence later was sold to the government and today contains the offices of the Bank of Thailand.

The entrance

Tula Bunnag's House

Tula Bunnag House
The main houses from the garden

Wall hangings

In 1963 Tula Bunnag, then an official in the Royal Household Department, began constructing a Thai-style house alongside a quiet klong on the outskirts of Bangkok. Using four teak wood houses from Ayudhya province about 80 years old, Tula arranged the house into a square and built a deck connecting all four. The family living quarters, religious shrine, and Tula's studio are situated on top while the dining area and cooking facilities are on the ground floor.

Small resident

Outside sitting area

On the terrace

Plants in the pond beneath the terrace

The owner on the ground level

Roof detail

Hok Lok Siaw House

Hok Lok Siaw House

A residence originally constructed in 1813 during the reign of Rama II (r. 1809-1824), the Hok Lok Siaw House is one of the relatively few fine examples of Chinese residential architecture in the city. The house was built by Phraya Srirajakorn, the father of Phraya Sampativanij, both prominent businessmen in early Bangkok. It was first constructed near the Chao Phraya River but was moved to its present site on Sathorn Road later and was modified somewhat by a French engineer in 1892. The Hok Lok Siaw House--standing for happiness, wisdom, and long life--is presently owned and resided in by Lalong Bunnag.

Window detail

The front

Reception room

The inner court yard

The Grand Palace

The buildings of the Grand Palace were begun by King Rama I (r. 1782-1809) immediately after he moved the capital of Siam across the Chao Phraya River from Thonburi to Bangkok. At one time or another each of the nine kings of the ruling Chakri Dynasty has slept within its walls although today His Majesty King Bhumibol Adulyadej resides at Chitrlada Palace.

Palace detail: symbol of the Chakri Dynasty

Monks in front of the Grand Palace

Lion's head detail

The Grand Palace is a colorful collection of court buildings, temples, and barracks. The dominating building is the Chakri Throne Hall, designed by the British architect John Chinitz. It was begun in 1876 and completed in 1882 and vividly reflects the eclectic tastes of the Siamese leaders in those days. The story goes that the conservative elders at court disliked the European style of the building and forced a compromise in architectural design; the result was a European structure with three Siamese-style spires on the roof. The throne hall on the second floor is where His Majesty receives the credentials of all envoys. King Rama V lived in a building behind the Chakri Throne Hall.

Elsewhere in the grounds of the Grand Palace is the small sala called Phra Thinang Sanam Chan which was constructed by Rama II and is renown for the single plank of wood which makes up the floor. The building behind it is the location of the ashes of Kings Rama I, II, and III and their consorts.

Close-up of the Chakri Hall

Front view of the Chakri Hall

Sala in the Palace

Potted plant

Ladies of the Court

Portuguese Embassy

Window detail

Coat of Arms of Portugal

Portugal was the first European kingdom to have official contact with Siam; these contacts date from 1511AD and were marked by exceptionally friendly relations over the centuries so much so that Portuguese men at arms were frequently employed by the kings of Ayudhya (1350-1767AD). King Rama I granted a piece of land to the King of Portugal in Bangkok in 1786 four years after the capital was moved from Thonburi across the river.

In 1820 King Rama II gave land to Portugal where a "Portuguese factory" and the residence of the first consul to Siam, Manuel da Silveira, were established. This property, 72 wah along the river, is the site of the present embassy, the oldest in Bangkok.

View from the river

Entrance

Government House

From the front lawn

Arched entrance

Detail

Certainly one of the most imposing residences in Bangkok is that constructed by King Rama VI for one of his most favored aides, Chao Phraya Ram Rakhob. This richly ornate building was later sold to the government and is today Government House, the office of the prime minister of Thailand and other government leaders.

Court yard at the back
of the Government House.

Ban Phitsanuloke

View from the garden

View from the front pond

Another ornate mansion given by King Rama VI to a favorite courtier was the house on Phitsanuloke Road known as Ban Phitsanuloke. It is currently the official residence of the prime minister of Thailand. This European-style residence was built for Phraya Anirudh Deva but later was sold to the government. The first official guest was the commander of Japanese forces attacking Southeast Asia in World War II.

Statue in the grounds

Pond and buildings behind the house

Roof detail

From the back pond

Seri Manangasila

Not far from Ban Phitsanuloke is
another major house from the Sixth Reign.
This is the Tudor-style Seri Manangasila,
now used as a government guest house

Wall painting at the Wang Lee House

Roof detail at the Wang Lee House

Utensils

74

Water scene

Inner courtyard of the Hok Lok Siaw house

Roof detail of Ban Pho Tale

Detail of building in the Grand Palace

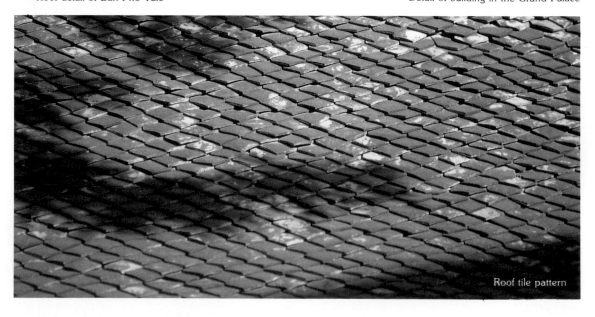

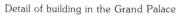
Roof tile pattern

78

Sala at Sukhothai Palace.

Roof detail of the Nai Lert House

Hanging plant

Palm backlit

Vachiravut College

A dormitory of Vachiravut College, formerly the Royal Pages School founded by King Rama VI, is patterned after the English public schools Eton and Harrow. The multi-colored dormitories are executed in classic Bangkok-period style.

From the playing field

Sala from the main house

Wall detail   Stone Ganesha

M.R. Kukrit Pramoj's House

A leading man of letters in Siam as well as a former prime minister, Kukrit Pramoj also possesses one of the most attractive Thai-style houses in the Kingdom. A series of old houses were dismantled, moved to their present site on Soi Suan Phlu and reconstructed along classical lines but also permitting air-conditioned 20th century living on the lower level. The oldest building is the sala, or meeting house, which was re-assembled in front of the main complex. The sala dates back about 170 years and originally was situated near the Giant Swing in the old part of Bangkok. Other houses were brought to Bangkok from Ayudhya province north of Bangkok.

Beautiful bonsai trees for which Kukrit is also well-known decorate the residence grounds and terraces and ancient stone carvings, especially some fine Khmer examples, lend a museum-like quality to the spacious manicured garden of the residence.

Overlooking the pond

Lamp

On the upper terrace

Prince Chula Chakrabongse's House

Front view

    This house on the banks of the Chao Phraya River not far from Wat Po (Temple of the Reclining Buddha) was given to the late Prince Chula Chakrabongse of Phitsanulok, the heir presumptive and Chief of the Army General Staff during the reign of Rama VI, by his mother, Queen Saowapaphongsri. The house was designed early in the 20th century by an Italian architect. It features a unique tower which closely resembles the "widow's walk" found in 19th century homes of American mariners in New England. The tower was designed to house Buddha images and to provide a vantage point on the river. The tower room still contains Buddha images.

Tower overlooking the river

Tower detail

Front view

Diplomatic Residences.

After Portugual, France has the best riverside embassy residence in Bangkok. Dating back to the mid-19th century, the present residence has retained considerable charm and grace despite numerous renovations and the presence of a massive modern hotel a few meters away.

The British forsook the Chao Phraya River as the site of their embassy in the early 1920's and struck out for the wilds of Ploenchit Road which was then well out of town. The famed colonial architect Sir Edward Luytens is credited with designing the embassy residence which still is a landmark among European buildings in the city.

The embassy of the Netherlands occupies a large secluded tract of land on Wireless Road next to a beautifully spacious klong. At one time the property of Prince Boworadet who sought unsuccessfully to lead a pro-monarchy counter-coup against the 1932 coup makers, the building has belonged to the Dutch since 1946.

Another old house on Wireless Road which became an embassy residence after World War II is that of the Americans. The old colonial-style building on Wireless Road was selected by the late Mrs. Edwin Stanton in 1946 when her husband became the first American ambassador to Thailand. At that time the building had suffered considerably during the war; the grounds were full of junked Japanese military equipment.

Netherlands

Netherlands

Denmark

French Embassy

British Embassy

British Embassy

British Embassy

American Ambassador's Residence

Old wooden building

Phra Suthi At-Narumontr's House

In the mid-1920's Phra Suthi At-Narumontr, a leading jurist and Siam's first Harvard Law School graduate, built a European - style home on klong-lined and tree-shaded Petchaburi Road. The house was located next to an older teak house built by his mother, Khunying Tad, in 1917. They are among the few old residences still found along old Petchaburi Road.

On the terrace

Woodwork detail of the old house

The "new" house seen from the old

Phraya Attakarn Prasit's House

View from the lawn

Entrance

One of more than 10 houses built by the late Phraya Attakarn Prasit on the soi (lane) which now bears his name, this house was built circa 1909 for family members. Phraya Attakarn served as Attorney General of Siam Under King Rama V and Rama VI.

Jim Thompson's House

Roof detail

One of Bangkok's art and architectural landmarks is the home of the late James H.W. "Jim" Thompson, an American silk dealer, who disappeared mysteriously while vacationing in Malaysia in 1966. Jim Thompson assembled an impressive collection of Asian art in his several decades in Siam and housed them in his Thai-style house on Klong Maha Nag. The house is assembled from parts of six old houses the oldest of which forms the main room and comes from a house originally built about 1800 in the nearby silk-weaving village of Bang Krua; the teak floor planks are about 14″ wide and 2″ thick. The rest of the houses are about 70 years old and come from Ayudhya province.

Jim Thompson began work on his house in 1958 and it was completed the following year. He bequeathed his house to his nephew, Henry B. Thompson III who formed the James Thompson Foundation. The house is now a museum and is open to the public. Its current occupant and unofficial curator is the crusty but genial William Riley who helps perpetuate the Jim Thompson legend.

From the klong

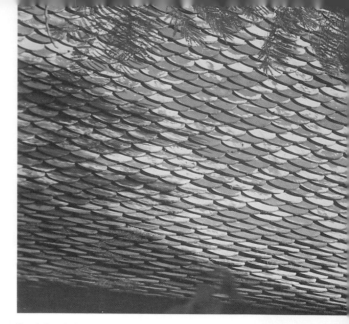

Roof detail

Front entrance

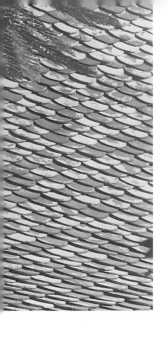

From the main house   Dvaravati sculpture

In the study

From the garden

104

Carved door

From the river

Krom Phra Chan Palace

The riverside Krom Phra Chan Palace is the family home of Her Majesty Queen Sirikit. The house was built around 1926 for the wedding of Her Majesty's father Mom Chao Nakkhatra Kitiyakara who was descended from Prince Chandaburi, the first son of King Rama V. The house was designed by the French architect Charles Béquelin. It is currently the residence of M.R. Kalyanakit Kitiyakara, Her Majesty's brother, and his wife Khunying Arun.

Garden party

Cooking utensils

Cooking on the lawn

Kamthieng House

Ox cart

Table setting

Roof detail

Roof detail

Roof detail

In the Siam Society grounds

Probably the finest example of northern-style Thai architecture in Bangkok is found on the grounds of the Siam Society, the 19th century Kamthieng House from Chiang Mai. The house originally belonged to a Nimmanheminda family member who exercised a tax monopoly on betel nut sold in the Chiang Mai area and was donated to the Siam Society in 1963 by Nang Kimhaw, a descendent of the original owner. The house today serves as an ethnological museum. It consists of several separate buildings including the granary and kitchen located near the main living area.

Sala on the klong
at Tula Bunnag's home

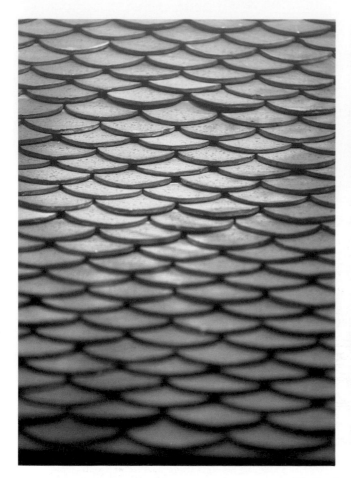

Tile detail   Jim Thompson's roof

Lotus

Kukrit Pramoj's birds

Government House

Dr. Piriya's driveway

Dr. Pleng's house

Professor Saeng Arun's Garden

Chao Phraya Arusi's house

Thai food at the house

M.R. Kukrit's home across the pond

The Wang Lee House

Roof detail

Detail

Inner courtyard

A fine old Chinese-style house located on the west bank of the Chao Phraya River, the Wang Lee family home today is surrounded by busy commercial enterprises along the busy riverfront. Although Chinese in shape and organization the house reflects some Western architectural influences in the details in a pleasing eclectic way.

Entrance

Wall painting

123

Phraya Prasert Subhakij's Residence

Entrance

In 1912 the Italian architect Annebale Rigotti designed a residence for Phraya Prasert Subhakij, the chamberlain of King Rama VI. The house was·executed in the style of an Italian villa. Later an addition was added on the east giving the house slightly more Thai flavor. Rigotti was a prolific architect in Bangkok designing inter alia the Parliament Building, Government House, and Ban Phitsanuloke. Today the house is owned by the grandson of Phraya Prasert, Dr. Piriya Krairiksh.

Front view

Side view

Front view

126

In the conservatory

Connie Mangskau's House

From the ▶

The Thai-style house of Connie Mangskau off Sukhumvit Road is a veritable museum of South - east Asian objets d'art housed in a series of old Thai houses reassembled in Bangkok. Although very traditional in design and furnishing the house is well-suited for modern entertaining on the up - stairs verandah.

Window

Ground Level

Main room

From the garden

On the verandah

Nai Lert's House

From the lawn

In 1893 Nai Lert (Phraya Phakdi Noraset) built the large multi-roofed house which today commands a large garden and pond on Wireless Road near Klong Saen Sap.

Roof detail

Sukhothai Palace

The palace with kite fliers

A residence in the palace

The palace and its symbol, a large jar

The Palace from Tamnak Nam

Tamnak Nam

Children on the lawn

Tamnak Daeng

The National Museum compound contains numerous buildings which house the art and historical treasures of the Kingdom. Not the least of these is the small red house, Tamnak Daeng, which was once the residence a queen of Rama I. It is one of the oldest residences remaining in Bangkok and has been completely restored.

House from the klong

Paul Berli's House

On a large lot on the outskirts of Bangkok, Paul Berli has reconstructed and renovated a large traditional Thai house which houses an extensive art collection. The surrounding gardens are filled with different types of palm trees, Mr. Berli's hobby.

From the lawn

Chartered Bank's House

Reflecting the pre-war European style of large homes in Bangkok, the residence of the Chartered Bank manager also boasts one of the most spacious gardens and lawns in land-tight Bangkok. This building was constructed in the early 1920's by the Anglo-Thai Company and passed into the hands of the Chartered Bank before World War II. It is one of the fine homes of Wireless Road.

Garden atmosphere

Window

Ancient City

Gateway to the old village

A mandatory stop outside Bangkok for anyone interested in the architecture, history, or culture of Siam is the Ancient City, a commercial enterprise dedicated to the restoration and preservation of Thai historical and cultural values. Set in a large green park roughly shaped like the Kingdom itself, the Ancient City has recreated, in smaller scale, the major temples and architectural achievements of Siam. Not the least among these recreations and restorations has been the re-establishment of many fine old houses, brought from upcountry sites to the Ancient City where they form new villages and markets in as authentic a re-creation as can be found in Siam.

Reconstructed house

Inside of the roof

On the steps of on old house

Ban Moh Palace

Entrance

From the side

Built during the reign of Rama III (r. 1824-1851), Ban Moh Palace has remained in the same family since the first owner, Prince Kunjara, a son of Rama II. It is one of the largest houses of its age left in Bangkok. During the reigns of Rama V and Rama VI the house was used to present Thai theatrical productions. The present owner is Mom Luang Chalaem Kunjara.

From the garden

Prince of Petchabun's Palace

Small house on a pond

Close view of the small house

These houses all belonged to the Prince of Petchabun. His widow Princess Boonchirathorn Juthathut still lives in one of them. The old house called Ruan Lomphat Chai Khao (Breezy House by the Hill) is next to a hill ordered built by King Rama IV more than 100 years ago. The house was built in 1925.

Large house on the pond

House on Sathorn Road

A good example of a surviving house on Sathorn Road owned by the Hong Kong and Shanghai Bank is this elegant home designed for life in the tropics before the days of air conditioning.

Lilypad on the klong

From the driveway

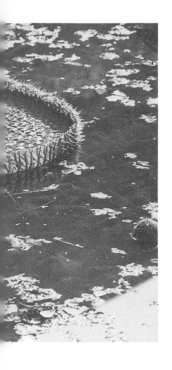

Side view

Dr. Vichai Posayachinda's House

Staircase

Roof

One of the most attactive, and inaccessible houses of Bangkok's Chinatown is the family home of Dr. Vichai Posayachinda. Although designed by an Englishman form Penang, this home combines European design with aspects of a Chinese home from the owner. No longer occupied, the house is reputedly haunted and is used as a shrine to the memory of earlier owners.

On ground level

157

Round window

Upper window

Roof lights

Inner courtyard

Tucked out of the way at Amphorn Gardens, no longer used and partially grown over by trees and weeds stands a fine old door which waits its turn for either restoration or destruction.

Lacquer panel

The Lacquer Pavilion at Suan Pakkad Palace

Ban Phitsanuloke from the front pond

Light on leaves

162

Part of Professor Saeng Arun's roof

M.R. Kukrit's garden from the house

163

Detail of the Chakri Hall in the Grand Palace

Sukhothai Palace

164

British Embassy residence

Small home on a klong

American Embassy residence

Upper level of M.R. Kukrit's house.

Chinese roof detail

Thai roof detail

Ornate spirit house

Wooden spirit house

Ho Phra Trai Pidok (Library)

Front view

Detail of window panels

Ho Phra Trai Pidok, Wat Rakhang

This building was originally the house of King Rama I before his accession to the throne. It was built probably in 1767 when, after the fall of Ayudhya, the King went to reside at Thonburi where he became a general under King Taksin. In 1768 he donated his house to Wat Rakhang, or Wat Bang Wa Yai as it was then known, a monastery next to his house compound. The house then served as "kutti" or living quarters for the monks for a number of years.

Soon after he ascended the throne in 1782 he ordered that this former residence be refurbished and converted into the monastery's library or Ho Phra Trai Pidok. The task was assigned to the young Crown Prince who later became King Rama II. The Prince, a monk at the time, was a renowned artist.

The fine carvings of the door panels and pediment are attributed to the Prince, while the interior panels were painted by the celebrated painters of the day, notably the well-known Phra Acharn Nark who was also monk-artist.

Of all the houses illustrated in this book, this is the most elaborate and the oldest on record in Bangkok.

Ruen Po Tale

A 90-year old farmhouse from Pichit Province in central Siam, this is a sala (hall) presently used by Spha "Teddy" Palasthira for entertaining in Bangkok. It is the smallest of the "standard" Thai houses, i.e. three wa two sok in length or about seven meters. A wa is the distance of an arm span and a sok is the distance from elbow to fingertip. The house is made from one or two logs of teak which were dried at the same time, an important factor in keeping tight joints when the house expands and contracts.

The house is built in eight standard sections, three on the back and front and one at each end. It is easily dismantled and re-assembled. The thatch roof is completely waterproof and will last five years. The unique Thai-style wooden fittings on the ends of the roof, called pan lom in Thai, afford not only a graceful appearance to the steep roof but protect the thatch against the wind.

The sloping doors and windows of the traditional Thai-style houses further add stability to the pre-fabricated dwellings. Building off the ground improved circulation of air through the building, kept inhabitants dry during the wet season when paddies were flooded, and provided cover for family animals such as buffaloes, pigs, and chickens.

From the garden

Interior of Ruen Pho Tale

Windvane

Thatched roof detail

Dr. Pleng Tienprasit's House

Turret detail

One of the delightful old "gingerbread" style Victorian homes off Silom Road is that of Dr. Pleng Tienprasit Sheltered from view from the street, the pink turreted 19th century home is preserved in fine detail inside while family life goes on in a more modern building connected to next door.

Professor Saeng-Arun Rattakasikorn House

Three old houses from Ayudhya province made up Professor Saeng-Arun's home. Dismantled in pieces, they were brought down the river in a boat and reassembled in the present compound near Sathorn Road. Originally the roofs were thatched, and these were replaced with tiles. The old wooden columns, rotted with age, also had to be replaced. The upper terrace around which the three houses are grouped was originally built in wood but eventually was replaced by concrete so that space underneath could be used as dining room and study. Otherwise, the structures have been meticulously preserved in their original form. Of special interest is a "yantra" or sacred symbol scribed on a bedroom door panel to protect the house from fire and other hazards. This "yantra" gives a date in the reign of King Rama V when the house was built. The house is located in a betel nut plantation so that it can only be approcahed through the palms and otlher vegetation.

The garden proper is upstairs in pots on the terrace which makes it typically Thai. The house is truly in an idyllic setting, a rare sight in the busy and congested metropolis.

Hanging pla

Roof detail

Three monkies

Tile work

House through the bamboo

From the klong

Rolf von Bueren's Houses

Von Bueren, who first came to Bangkok in 1962, is another expatriot who has made this country his home, more, who has decided to live it the traditional way. He began building his house in the late' 60's for his family in a compound on Sukhumvit Soi (lane) 23. The beginning was a modest collection of decorative parts. But soon old houses from the country were brought to be re-assembled in the compound. Now there are several Thai houses: his own sala, a dining pavilion converted from a Northern Thai rice barn standing in a pond, a guest house, a new wing for children, and a group of houses for rent. The photographs here show one of the rented houses which became the residence of The Count and Countess de Salis in 1981 - 3. Standing on tall stilts and open wooden terrace, the ground floor is relatively open except for a study and a service area. The Count and the Countess, like Rolf von Bueren, have become devoted to the Thai way of life, and the old national flag of Siam (the elephant flag) flying over their entrance sala (pavilion) announces this cultural allegiance.

Entrance

Upper terrace

Entrance pavili

Sitting area upstairs

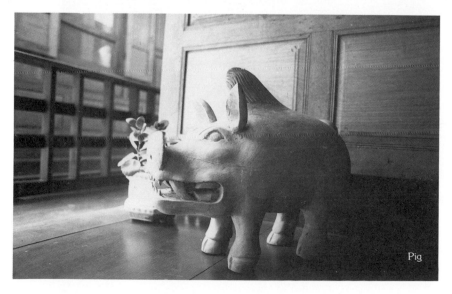

Pig

Entrance pavilion

spirit house

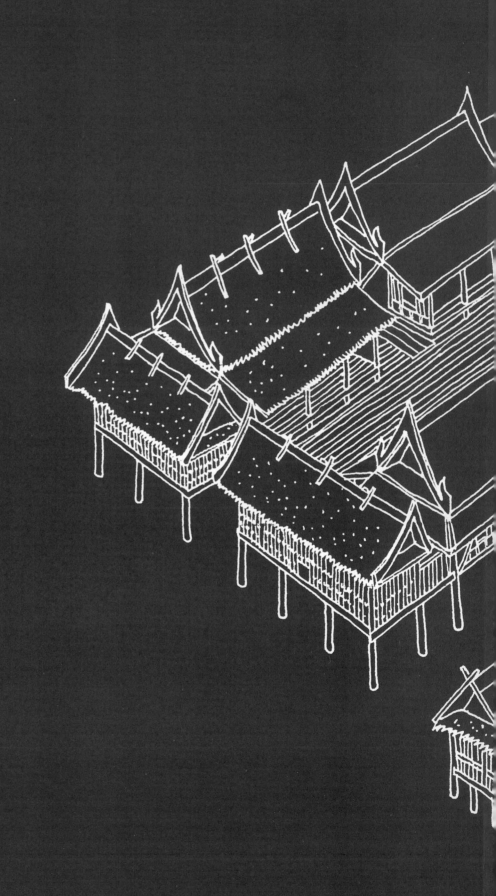